300 Plus

Teacher Hacks

and Tips

Edited by

Debra Chapoton

ISBN: 9781798767610

Printed in the USA

Also available in the Kindle bookstore with live links, free with the purchase of this book.

Foreword

Here you'll find over 300 tips and hacks, as well as advice and warnings, curated from hundreds of teachers and multiple educational forums. The ideas are not divided by age level or subject matter since most educational concepts can be adapted to fit specific classes. What may seem specifically geared to a kindergarten classroom may, for some teachers, be an idea that with a little tweaking fits perfectly in a high school math class. Or a tip for secondary teachers may inspire an early education professional to create something to use with a second grade class. You never know. Read all the tips and hacks and use what's best for you.

They are arranged in the following categories:

Chapter One

Your Personal Classroom

Tricks and Tips

1. Turn your table top into a dry erase board.

A roll of dry-erase contact paper will do the trick. This is great for working with a small group of kids and drawing out whatever lesson you're on. Two, three, four or five students (plus you sometimes) at a round (or rectangle or kidney shaped) table able to plot out subject matter without the limitations of an 8 x 11 piece of paper will amaze you.

You might want to get permission to cover all the student desks as well. Imagine the possibilities.

2. Use photo boxes to organize and store tasks. Print the tasks on a card or use an actual photo. Stuff stays organized and they're easy to pull out for work stations.

3. Instead of numbering devices (tablets, headsets, whiteboards, etc.) with sticky labels that peel off, use permanent marker or, for items with screens, make the screen saver a photo of you or your students holding a card with the item's number.

4. Use microfiber cloths on dry erase boards. If you're particularly crafty, sew them into mitts to fit on little or big hands.

5. Color code the Chromebooks or tablets with different colored or print tape or glitter tape. Match the tape on the cords, side of book, and storage spot.

6. Need to color code something else? Grab a bunch of paint sample strips from the big box store.

7. Avoid the noise and interruption of pencil sharpening by having two small pails, one marked "ready to write" filled with sharp pencils and the other marked "please sharpen" where a student can drop his dull one, grab a good one and get back to his/her seat.

8. Hot glue personal decorations to your desk (family photos, a flower vase) so they don't get bumped off. Scrape off at end of year and breakables stay intact.

9. Put command hooks on the backs of chairs so germ-phobe kids can hang purses and bags.

10. Use a pool noodle for a door stop.

11. Organize papers with magazine racks.

12. Velcro white board markers near the top of the board, where kids can't reach them, tip down to stay fresh.

13. When you throw out used markers and glue sticks, save the caps to replace those that are inevitably misplaced or lost.

14. Mount a "rear view mirror" on the board so you can have eyes in the back of your head.

15. Glue a small clock to the clipboard you use to keep track of time without having to glance at the wall clock.

16. Use hangers and binder clips to store bulletin board pieces in clear plastic—you can see what's what at a glance.

17. Use cheap black gloves to clean dry erase boards.

18. Make a slant board by flipping a 3 ring binder inside out and clipping it together with a binder clip.

19. Use clip art and print in poster size to make your bulletin boards dazzling. Use Adobe.

20. Help yourself to some free Priority USPS boxes from the post office to make your own book boxes with monkey glue and duct tape. Decorate or spray paint.

21. Put up a QR code at Open House so parents can access your contact information on their phones.

22. Use either double sided tape or else use hot glue over painter's tape when taping things to the wall.

23. Scotch makes outdoor mounting tape for heavier items.

24. Keep hand sanitizer on your desk with a rubber band around its neck so it gives smaller squirts.

25. Shoe boxes make storage neat. Check shoe store for empties and hit up family and friends for extras.

Chapter Two

Homework

Guidelines and Pointers

26. Having trouble getting kids to hand in homework? Make a racetrack on a poster board with a lane for each horse. Student teams of four represent a different horse. The horse moves ahead one space each time all four turn their homework in. This eliminates any individual from public shame, but uses a bit of peer pressure to build a good habit.

27. Vary the types of homework you give.

Examples are: practice for retention, critical and abstract thinking, hands on skills, problem-solving, creation or project-oriented, question and answer, and reading. There are many more types, of course, but this is a reminder to check that you aren't giving the same (boring) type.

28. Don't make homework busy work. For example word searches can have a goal of mastering recognition of words (especially for foreign languages), but aren't necessarily learning tools or a good use of homework time.

30. Make sure you know your school's policy so you don't give too much or too little.

31. Homework should be meaningful.

32. Homework should be purposeful and free of errors on your part.

33. Homework should be doable without parental input.

34. Always do the homework yourself before making copies for kids. You're bound to find some typos, missing lines, or confusing instructions.

35. Don't give more homework than you can correct and return the following day. A good way to stay on top of things is to have certain (practice-type) assignments graded as credit or no credit. Quickly walk the room and check off whether it's done or not as you orally go over the answers.

36. Some student work requires specific feedback from you. If you have five classes turning in lengthy assignments, cycle through the students giving more feedback to one class this time and a different class next time. You don't have to grade everything every time.

37. Have students grade each other's papers. This can often be a learning experience for them as they see things from a different perspective.

38. Use technology to grade only on occasion. It's so easy to feed the multiple choice sheets through a machine and poof they're graded, but life doesn't always work that way.

Chapter Three

Quieting the Room

Instructions and Commands

39. Tell students to pop an imaginary marshmallow in their mouths. It's hard to talk with your mouth full. After the first time you can just say, "Pop a marshmallow, guys," and puff out your own cheeks. Most students (early elementary) will follow suit.

40. If you like electronics, consider the Super Sound Box or Class Dojo or the Too Noisy App which detects noise level and signals when voices become too loud.

41. Make silence a group game by announcing "silent 20" as a way to conclude activities. If kids are seated and quiet in 20 seconds (you're counting them off) then the class advances a square on a one of those old game boards you've collected from garage sales. When they reach the last square (weeks? months? later) they get the reward of a (popcorn, candy, or pizza) party.

42. Greet students at the door and remind them that today will be an especially (medium, giant, crazy) quiet day.

43. Invent or borrow a catchy slogan or refrain whereby you say the first part and the students respond with the second. Examples:
Teacher: "Oh Mickey, you're so fine." Students: "You're so fine, you blow my mind. Hey Mickey." (You could substitute the name of the loudest student.)
Teacher: "The best students are ..." Students: "... the quiet ones."

44. Instead of saying "Stop talking, turn around, get your book out and turn to page ..." try starting with "Eyes on me" and wait a beat for them to comply, then you can give them the page number or whatever.

45. Keep consequences as small as possible when rules are broken. Increase the penalty only if necessary.

46. Match penalties to students. For some being kicked out of class is a reward, for others appearing dumb in front of their peers is more humiliating than they can handle.

47. Use humor. Throwing in a question like "what's the best way to embarrass a superhero" on a test eases tension.

48. Never punish the entire class, it annoys the good students and the culprits aren't singled out and feel they got away with something.

49. Build content-related anticipation by announcing what they'll be learning today.

50. Try to state a summary of what was learned today or have a student do it at the end of class.

51. Curb complainers by requiring them to sing a line from your favorite happy song. (Walking on sunshine, wo-oh) (Because I'm happy) (I can make your hands clap.)

52. Ramp up your own enthusiasm. Remember you are touching and changing the future of this world.

53. Remember, you're their teacher. You're not their friend or their mother or their father or their jailer. You can be friendly and motherly and fatherly though, and you can be strict without being mean.

54. If you have to kick a kid out of class, remind him that he gets a fresh start tomorrow when all will be forgiven.

55. Make classroom rules and goals clear by posting them on the front wall.

56. Address behavior issues immediately without anger if possible.

57. Build extra things into your lesson plans. There's nothing worse than a class with nothing to do and five minutes left before the bell rings. Have review questions or quick games handy.

58. Schedule one on one time to talk with students.

59. Develop student-led activities and lessons. The best way to learn is to teach so let them take the reins at times.

60. Criticize problems not students.

Chapter Four

Things you Shouldn't Say or Do

Advice and Warnings

61. Never say, "You have potential, but you're not living up to it." It's all right to say the first part, but leave it at that.

62. Never say, "Your brother/sister was a better student." Who wants to be compared to their sibling? Go ahead and say nice things about the brother or sister, but stay away from comparisons.

63. Never say, "You'll never amount to anything." Of course, that might motivate some kids to work harder and show you how wrong you are, but more likely you'll just lose their respect and any chance of reaching them.

64. Never say, "What's wrong with you?" Better to say something like "How are you feeling today? Is there something I need to know?" Start a dialogue not a rant.

65. Never say, "Why can't you do it right?" Learn to use the word "yet" as in "You're not getting it yet, but you will."

66. Never say, "Don't you ever stop talking?" You'll just get a smart answer back and probably a snarly look. Try saying something positive instead.

67. Never say, "I'm busy now, ask me later." A kid with a question is your number one priority. Maybe other kids have the same question. Stop what you're doing and answer, even if you've answered that exact question twice already.

68. Never say, "Who do you think you are?" That sounds like you've lowered yourself to their level. You're the adult; make statements.

69. Never say, "Everybody else understands, why don't you?" Way to make a kid feel inferior and be a jerk. Instead say, "How about you see me later and we'll go over it together."

70. Never say, "What did you just say to me?" Asking him to repeat something awful gets everyone's attention. Better to say, "Don't you ever say that to me again."

71. Never use foul language or inappropriate slang.

72. Don't give full on body contact hugs. (No kisses either!)

73. Don't invite students to your home.

74. Don't give students rides.

75. Don't meet students at restaurants, bowling alleys, etc.

76. Don't bad mouth another teacher or agree with a student's negative assessment of another teacher (or administrator).

77. Dress like a teacher, not a student. If you can see through it, up it, or down it, don't wear it.

78. Don't gossip about the students, the parents, or the teachers.

79. Make sure your attire and actions and behaviors are G rated out in public in the community in which you teach.

80. Never say "I don't care if my students like me or not," because you know that's a lie.

81. Never say, "That's a stupid question."

82. Never say, "I've already gone over that. Weren't you listening?" Kids process things differently. Don't embarrass him.

83. Teachers should never sit for the entire class period. Five minutes maybe, but teaching is done on your feet.

84. Don't run to an administrator for every little thing. Be independent.

85. Don't eat your lunch or drink coffee during class.

86. When kids say "I can't do this," you repeat it and add the word "yet." "You can't do this … yet."

Chapter Five
Discipline

Dos and Don'ts

87. Your highest priority is to form relationships with each and every student.

88. Give them space. Avoid edging yourself into their personal space. You wouldn't like it either.

89. Be on the lookout for positive things. Acknowledge them.

90. Be sincere. Kids can spot a phony or a suck-up same as you can.

91. Kids will remember how you made them feel over what you taught them. Make them feel good about your class.

92. Find a teacher who can mentor you. Later, after ten years of experience, be a mentor for a new teacher.

93. Choose to be happy.

94. Get enough sleep. Why is this under discipline? Because if you're tired you'll snap. We don't want that.

95. Be clear about expectations and rules as well as penalties and punishments.

96. Try to handle the less serious situations in the classroom without involving the administration.

97. A wordless glare can be punishment enough for some kids.

98. Verbal reprimands need to be brief and immediate. If they can also be given privately that's the best.

99. Acknowledge positive behavior with kind words.

100. Be fair and impartial. The rules are for everyone. No exceptions.

101. Don't give a warning, then another, then not give any consequence if the student doesn't improve.

102. Don't threaten a consequence you're not willing to follow through or one that is ridiculous, illegal, or unreasonable.

Chapter Six:

Lesson Planning

Live and Learn

103. Use colors to differentiate categories as you plan. Use colored pencils if you like to handwrite or the highlight feature in Word if you print your plans. Examples: blue for explanations, yellow for quizzes, red for tests, green for homework, pink for games, purple for reading, orange for classroom participation, etc.

104. Make lesson plans for complete units or chapters. Don't do one day at a time and hope you'll cover everything you need to by the end of the semester or year.

105. Expect to spend two hours of planning for every hour of class time.

106. Research and learn (if they didn't teach this in your education classes) about the different learning styles and incorporate those styles into every lesson. In other words don't leave out the visual or spatial learner, the auditory learner, the kinesthetic learner, the musical learner, the linguistic learner, etc.

107. Make your step by step plans on the computer. You should have 8 -10 things per hour. Print your daily plans out for your lesson plan book and also print them on 3 x 5 cards so you can have something in your hand or on your clipboard (seating chart) for reference.

108. Put a general routine into each lesson, i.e same beginning and ending routine (handing back papers, starting homework), but vary the middle with a five to ten or fifteen minutes each of explanatory teaching, oral or written practice, audio or video reinforcement, and multiple other interaction patterns like using manipulatives, taking quizzes, doing a quick game, singing a song, or memorizing a formula.

109. Connect with other teachers and share plans. Is there a curriculum calendar you have to follow? What's the bigger picture? Is your district objective-based, test-focused, or looking at shorter-term goals?

110. Don't rely on "fluff" or fun stuff. You can build fun things in, but zero in on activities that provide the richest rewards, are relevant and rigorous.

111. Work backwards. What's your goal? What will be on the test? If you start thinking about what you want to accomplish first, the puzzle will put itself together.

112. Relate your lessons to real life whenever possible.

113. Be flexible and put more into your plans than you think you can accomplish. It's better to have too much material than not enough. You can make adjustments the next day.

114. Poll your students' aptitudes and learning styles early in the year and teach accordingly. There are multiple intelligences—teach to them.

115. Don't wait until Sunday night to do your lesson plans.

116. It's okay to find and use lesson plans that come with text books or you find online, but you will always, always, have to adapt them to your style and your classes.

Chapter Seven

Classroom Management

Supervision and Control

117. Make laminated signs to keep things on track. A "NO QUESTIONS" sign turned outward signals a time for keeping those pesky kids away from your desk. Other ideas for signs are:

ESPAÑOL

ENGLISH

QUIET

TEST TOMORROW
TEST TODAY

118. Glue fuzzy black pom poms to the ends of those fat dry erase markers for quick erasing ease.

119. Use clothespins as pencil grippers for young kids having trouble with fine motor skills.

120. Wrap your classroom pencils in glitter tape so you won't lose your whole supply the first month. Easy to spot and ask for returns.

121. Use decorated clothespins to hang work. Paint them and/or write encouraging slogans on each one:
Be truthful
Stay strong
You are smart
Believe in yourself
Be true to your friends
You make me happy, etc.

122. Write your students' names on Popsicle sticks and stick in a jar. Pull them out to call on people randomly.

123. Dump a bottle of Elmer's Glue onto a sponge. Every few weeks, flip them and give them a spritz of water, and use them instead of glue sticks.

124. Have students use hand signals for interruptions such as 1 finger up for off-subject question, 2 fingers to get up to sharpen pencil or get a tissue, 3 fingers to go to the bathroom.

125. Got a restless middle or high school class? Everybody up. It's a 30 second dance party. Make them imitate (mock) you and your classic jive moves.

126. Got a restless elementary class? Take a 10 minute stretch and chat break.

127. Keep a "class mascot" (could be anything from a ball to a stuffed animal to a picture of them smiling) on your desk. When the class needs to refocus or calm down hold up the mascot.

128. Got projects going? Divide the supplies into 4 or 5 bins placed around room. This eliminates a lot of foot traffic and crowding.

129. Keep all your substitute teacher materials and emergency plans in one large bin or deep desk drawer or filing cabinet, clearly labeled.

130. Keep a "personal emergency" drawer full of toiletries like deodorant, cologne, mouthwash, toothbrush & paste, and sanitary supplies. Also stock a spare shirt & pants, even socks and shoes (you never know).

131. Keep a folder of busy work that can be quickly handed out in the event you have to leave the class unexpectedly. Stomach flu, anyone?

132. Give "shout-outs" every day, targeting different students at the end of the hour/day with positive words of encouragement or praise. "Hey, Audrey, that was a clever comment you made earlier." "Marco, you always make me laugh. Thanks." "Good job on your test, Charlotte."

133. Low participation? Try giving out "tickets" for an end of week raffle. Prizes could be anything from candy to a 5 minute head start on the next test.

135. Don't make students read aloud in the large group (whole class) if they don't want to.

136. Don't give up on any student. Everyone can learn.

137. Don't stop your lesson for minor infractions. Learn when to ignore the small stuff.

138. Never yell. Once you yell you've lost the battle. Usually a lower, slower voice is more threatening and better heeded.

139. Don't give control over to the students. Don't let them sway you to postpone a test or forgo the homework. You're the one making decisions, not them. If you make that kind of change, let them know it's your decision and the reason why.

140. Don't show favoritism. Just don't.

141. Don't be inconsistent whether it's grading or rules or accepting late work or marking tardies.

Chapter Eight

Garage Sale Finds

Bargains and Steals

142. Repurpose an old spice rack for small items: tacks, paper clips, safety pins, rubber bands, etc.

143. A clothes drying rack works great for clipping art work to.

144. Wireless doorbell—great for getting attention.

145. Rolling cart—store stuff and move it easily around the room as needed.

146. Roomba—keeps the floor clean and teaches a little technology. AKA the classroom pet.

147. Shoe rack—the possibilities are endless. Collect homework, cell phones, store items, etc.

148. Leggos—use for games

149. Soap dispensers—store paint, squeeze out as needed.

150. Cookie jar—use for suggestions or to pull out their names for oral participation or to store miscellaneous items.

151. Toothbrush holders—make great wet paintbrush holders.

152. Melamine or shower board panels make cheap whiteboards.

153. Old DVD cases also work as smaller whiteboards.

154. Mardi Gras beads can decorate the bulletin board or be worn as a symbol (classwork done, winning team, etc.).

155. Use chalk board paint to make furniture finds useful.

156. Shoe organizers make headphone storage easy.

157. Jewelry holders make nice storage hacks for washi tape, etc.

158. Old tennis balls—slit them and slip them on chair legs to eliminate squeaky annoying chair sliding noises.

159. Bath mats can be seating spots for special groupings.

160. Somebody's kitchen or bedroom curtains may be just the thing you need to hide clutter. Wash, dry, and hang with clips or duct tape.

161. Canvas work aprons make seat sacks to hang on the back of students' chairs.

162. Seat cushions from summer wicker chairs can be mounted on crates for clever and mobile seats.

163. Longer wicker cushions can fit over several crates forming a bench with storage.

164. An old wine rack can be painted and repurposed as a holder for various supplies.

165. The boards from Monopoly, Sorry, and other games that require tokens to move spaces can be mounted on the wall and used to mark off advances that lead to parties or rewards of some kind.

Chapter Nine
Dollar Store Finds

Treasures and Novelties

166. Bingo dabbers—for art projects, decorating, even for quick colored grading.

167. Clear jar—suggestion jar, question jar, game choices, etc.

168. Alphabet stickers—put on plastic bottle caps and use as manipulatives.

169. Plastic party plates that have three compartments—use them for math manipulatives. Dry erase markers work on these too.

170. A string of white Christmas lights in a glass jar and you've made your own relaxing mood lighting for a special class day.

171. Slip writing assignments into plastic sleeve protectors and have students use dry erase markers to make corrections and comments on others' writings.

172. Wear kitty ears, a tiara, a sombrero, or whatever you can find for those times in class when you want to be invisible. Explain that when you're wearing that item it means they must problem-solve on their own and you're free to work in small groups or with individuals or quietly at your desk.

173. Get a clear plastic jar or bin for a cell phone jail.

175. Multiple cookie sheets stacked crisscross one on top of the other allow air flow to dry art work that will sit safely on each tray.

176. Keep bathroom passes less germy by inserting them in a plastic holder and attaching a key ring with a stretchy coiled bracelet.

177. Store small manipulatives in cupcake size plastic containers.

178. Keep an "Absent Work Bin" of files folders labeled by class period and containing work with the absent student's name on it.

179. Stack cheap crates to use as shelves.

180. Recover ugly storage boxes (FedEx, UPS, Amazon) with decorative duct tape.

181. Plastic table cloths make durable bulletin board coverings.

182. Get some clear nail polish to go over markings that tend to wear off quickly.

183. Leftover Easter egg dye can be used to color clothes pins, Popsicle sticks, etc.

184. Cheap vegetable oil can be used to unclog glue caps.

185. Velcro strips can be used on carpet to mark seating spots, games, etc.

187. A disposable turkey roasting pan makes a good homework tray.

188. Hair conditioner makes it easy to wash dirty paint brushes.

189. The smallest plastic containers (with tops) make it safe to shake dice without them flying across the room.

190. Large clear cookie jar can be filled with classroom prizes.

191. Hula hoops and pool noodles: cut up the noodles and put them on the hoop to make giant round math manipulatives.

192. Face scrubbers can be used as whiteboard erasers.

193. A cheap silverware holder makes a decent desk drawer organizer.

194. Ink stamp kits. Mark students' papers with a variety of stamps from letters to pictures to symbols.

195. Buy up the sticker books. These are worth their weight in gold. Some kids will do anything for stickers.

Chapter Ten
Make Your Own Games

Contests and Competitions

196. Make a game with dry erase dice. Write short questions on each side. If you want to make the dice permanent use clear nail polish to set. Roll and play. Examples for various subject areas:

English: WHAT IS THE PLOT? WHO WAS THE VILLAIN?

Spanish: ¿CÓMO TE LLAMAS? ¿CUÁNTOS AÑOS TIENES?

Math: 2 X 5, 7 X 6

Social Studies: NAME 3 PRESIDENTS. WHAT IS THE CAPITAL

OF OHIO?

197. Repurpose BINGO into a lesson specific review game. Kids take on some of the work by cutting out the squares you've prepared and gluing them over the numbers. Then you call out clues instead of letters/numbers and they cover the corresponding square. This works well in foreign language with pictures of vocabulary. The same concept works for math (call out multiplication or division problems), science (periodic table), history (standards-based facts), and language arts (vocabulary or character/plot points). After you play get those cards laminated and you've got a long-lasting game. Be sure to label the container.

198. The game of MEMORY is easy to make and is similar to the BINGO construction in the previous hack except you make the squares larger and add a small matching number in the corner of each pair. You can make images with words, states with their capitals, math problems with their answers, etc.

199. AROUND THE WORLD is a simple game where students compete against the kid behind them. If he beats that kid he moves on, if he loses he takes that seat. The object is to get around the classroom and back to his own seat. You come up with the questions or flashcards.

200. Make your own JEOPARDY review game at
http://www.superteachertools.us/jeopardyx/

201. Create a scavenger hunt or "road rally" where kids team up and follow clues you've created. You might get other teachers to help you out by allowing your kids to enter their rooms for clues you've put there as well as other obvious spots around the school. This takes a lot of planning, but once made it can be brought out year after year.

202. PICTIONARY. You've already got the whiteboard and markers. Now make a vocabulary or phrase list and divide the class into teams. 30 second timer starts now.

203. FAMILY FEUD doesn't need a survey first. This game works well at the end of the year after lots of facts have been memorized like state capitals, bodies of water, presidents, authors, titles, etc. Simply write the category on an index card and list 5 items. Divide the class into families and start the fun.

204. Remember the rules for $100,000 PYRAMID, WHO WANTS TO BE A MILLIONAIRE, and WHEEL OF FORTUNE? You can make classroom versions specific to what you want to practice, review, or test just the same as the preceding hack.

205. Need a quick time killer for the last 5 minutes of class? Everybody stand up and line up from the front wall to the back wall. You've got ten seconds, go! Now you've got one minute to rearrange yourselves alphabetically by first name A at the back. Done? Now alphabetize by last name. What? There's still time left? Okay, rearrange yourselves from oldest to youngest. (More time? Try January to December birthdays, height, hair length or whatever else you can think of.)

206. POINTS FOR THE WIN is the simplest and most effective review game. Divide the class into two or more teams and simply ask questions that will be on the test. Keep score on the board.

207. Individualized POINTS FOR THE WIN is the same game, but no teams. Give each kid a mini whiteboard. You ask the question, they write the answer and quickly hold the board up. 2 points for the first person with the right answer, 1 point for everyone else who is right. Kids keep track of their own scores.

208. RACE TO THE BOARD is a team game that works well if your class sits in rows. Each row is a team. First person holds the marker (chalk in the old days). You ask the first question and the front seat kids can either run to the board to write the answer or pass the marker back until someone who knows the answer runs up. This as with most

games doesn't need a prize for the winners. Usually winning is its own reward.

209. FOUR HEADS ARE BETTER THAN ONE is a group based contest. Hand out a set of questions or problems to be answered or solved by the group in a set amount of time. Ring a bell to end the contest and go over the answers.

210. Double the excitement of team games that are evenly matched by having the winning team of each round add an X of O to a tic-tac-toe board you've drawn on the whiteboard. They don't get their point until they win at tic-tac-toe.

211. THUMB BALL is played with the kids sitting in a circle on the floor if you have room or at their seats. Take a large light colored beach ball (or big balloon) and mark it off into lots of sections. Fill each section with a question or problem. Students close their eyes and toss the ball. Whoever catches it must answer the question that their right thumb is touching. No points here; this is just for fun or review.

212. TEAM BUILDING isn't a game exactly, but might be used in upper secondary classrooms, sociology, for example. Students huddle in groups of five and work on a list of all the things they have in common. After a set amount of time teams reveal their lists and all

41

groups check off the number of total commonalities. Discussion follows.

213. RANDOM QUESTIONS needs a lot of input from kids. You need two jars, one for the questions and one for students' names to call on. You make up several questions like "Who's your favorite actor and why?" "What was your weirdest dream?" "What makes you gag?" "What animal creeps you out?" and ask them when you have a few minutes left at the end of class. Mix in some actual lesson-related questions. Leave blank strips of paper available for kids to add their own questions to the question jar. Be sure to preview the questions.

Chapter Eleven

Personnel

Go Along and Get Along

214. Make friends with the secretaries and the custodians and all the support staff.

215. Set discipline rules on the first day and stick with them.

216. Be consistent.

217. Use humor. Sarcasm works with older students.

218. Take advice from everyone.

219. Work smarter, not harder.

220. Make parent/teacher open house and conferences fun and exciting.

221. Wear comfortable clothing, especially shoes.

222. Don't listen to negative teachers.

223. Don't give free time. Make every minute count.

224. Pay attention to and follow school and district rules, goals, missions, and objectives. But keep your sanity. You can't do everything all the time.

225. Want to be the teacher with the highest attendance at open house? Create a "secret game" with students: extra credit if they come with their parents and give you the secret signal when they enter. The secret signal could be a word or gesture or something drawn on their hand (which they wave at you) or a folded note with their name and three things they learned today.

226. Stand in the hall between classes (secondary schools). See and be seen. Chat and observe.

227. Be an advisor for a club or coach a team.

228. Go to school events. Participate as needed. If you help another teacher chaperon kids on a field trip, you can bet you'll need his/her help at some point and he/she will be there for you.

Chapter Twelve

Technology Hacks

Techy Tips

229. Use an app like <u>Noise Down</u> to alert you when the decibel level is too high.

230. Use a battery operated light (touch to turn on or off) at a station near the door along with a sign out sheet and the pass to the bathroom. Students sign out, grab the pass and hit the light. No one else can leave if the light is on.

231. Use the app <u>Classdojo.com</u> so parents can keep up with their kids.

232. <u>Buzzmob.com</u> lets parents and teachers connect on a private network.

233. <u>Collaborizeclassroom.com</u> allows parents, students, and teachers discuss topics, trends, and student progress.

234. <u>Remind: School Communication</u> in the Apple App Store lets teachers send text messages to the entire class on the fly.

235. ITunes has <u>TeacherKit</u>. Use this app to take attendance, track grades, behaviors, allergies, and health issues for multiple classes.

236. <u>Google Apps for Education</u> is a free suite of productivity tools. Check it out.

237. <u>News-O-Matic</u> is a daily newspaper just for students.

238. <u>ONLYOFFICE</u> by Ascensio Systems is a cloud and on-site document management system.

239. <u>Book Creator</u> app allows even elementary school students to produce books with images, videos and audio.

240. <u>Nearpod</u> allows teachers to create digital lesson plans, share them with students and track progress.

241. <u>Socrative Teacher</u> allows teachers to gather data and assess their students and export that data.

242. <u>Explain Everything Whiteboard</u> presents information to students in a visually engaging manner.

243. <u>Edmodo</u> is a social media network for school.

244. <u>Bee-Bot</u> teaches young children control, directional language, and programming.

245. <u>Mathletics Student</u> lets kids compete with children all over the world.

246. <u>Comic Life</u> engages reluctant readers.

247. <u>iMovie</u> can be used to tell stories using digital media.

248. <u>Memrise</u>: learn languages free. Expand your vocabulary imaginatively.

249. Popplet can be used to create, organize and share.

250. Quizlet manages more than 13 million user-created flashcard sets on different topics.

251. Notability is a versatile app for note-taking.

252. Showbie is an assignment submission tool.

253. Show My Homework is a simple app for completing homework.

254. EKID is an augmented reality app that enables young children to explore the world by use of augmented flash cards.

255. Typesy - Keyboarding Program and Typing Tutor. The name says it all.

257. BEHCA Behavior Tracker. Also self-explanatory.

258. Studyo is a central hub for student assignments and tests.

259. Kiddom helps teacher plan, deliver, and assess.

260. Datability is for special education teachers to record and access data easily.

261. Smoovie Stop Motion is an app for stop motion animation.

262. Tame Your Thought Monster is an app designed to deal with fear, anxiety, etc., and to promote better behavior.

263. PSA App keeps parents updated about school events.

264. Boom Cards lets you create interactive quizzes and use other teachers' quizzes.

265. iCare Kids is an app for schools to provide information about their events as well as individual students.

266. iCare Teachers provides a data recording and communication platform between nurseries and parents.

267. The NEO LMS (Learning Management System) has features such as classes, assignments, grade book, lesson plans, chat rooms and more.

268. FlixREMIX allows you to annotate over a film with a commentary, set up questions, or explain things.

269. SMART Vocabulary is an app to grow and refine a student's vocabulary to prep for college entrance exams.

270. Use KAHOOT.it create interactive quizzes and track scores.

271. The Zip Grade app replaces Scantron machines as you use your phone to scan and grade instantly.

272. SHOW MY HOMEWORK is a school-wide service app for administering and monitoring homework.

273. Reading Trainer helps students improve reading efficiency.

274. Typing Fingers is an app for younger children to learn keyboarding.

275. CoSpaces creates 3D worlds for creative lessons.

276. Inspire - Flash Cards by Gamer Parents is an app that interrupts kids on their devices, targeting those who spend too much time on digital screens.

277. <u>Ergobreak 4 Kids</u> is an app to teach kids better posture and helps them remember and employ healthy computer habits.

278. <u>Study Flash</u> is a flash card revision tool for students and teachers with multiple options: text, audio, pictures, and in-app sharing.

279. <u>GCSEPod - Education on Demand</u> is an app and a gateway to an array of other learning and revision materials.

Chapter Thirteen

Non-techy Hacks

Old School Make-Do

280. Punch a long needle tack through a clothes pin to attach it to the bulletin board. Now you can hang things easily and change them out quickly.

281. Use wire storage racks to hang from bottom of cupboards. Place tissue boxes in upside down to dispense tissues more easily.

282. If you want to hot glue things to the walls, protect them first with painter's tape.

283. Plastic plates make good dry erase boards.

284. Glue a stapler to the wall where students can use it, but not move it.

285. Make a clipboard stand by gluing the clipboard to a picture frame that comes with a stand.

286. Use a dish drying rack to organize file folders on your desk. (The silverware holder is perfect for pens, pencils, etc.)

287. Write motivational slogans on your lending pencils such as "You are phenomenal" "You are unique" "You are amazing".

288. Write objectives on ping pong balls. Can you think of a way to use these?

289. Fill a shoe box with the cardboard toilet paper rolls which will separate markers from pens from pencils from paint brushes.

290. Hang a clothes pin near the entry door under a sign that says "No Name" and attach any papers that were turned in without a name.

291. Velcro small square pillows to the bottom of classroom chairs. For reading time the students tip them over and they become angled lounges.

292. Cut fat straws and duct tape them to student desks to keep pencils and pens from rolling around.

293. IF you put desks or tables in groupings and don't want them to pull apart, put the conjoining legs into a coffee can. That will keep them together and projects won't fall between the table top edges.

294. Reminder notes to go home with younger children work great as bracelets quickly glued, taped, or stapled around wrists as they leave the room. The short message can be written on one piece of paper 25 - 30 times, cut into strips, then voila. The parents may even send notes back this way.

295. Tape a zip lock bag to the edge of each desk on days when they'll be doing projects with lots of cutting, waste, or small pieces. A quick swipe pushes the mess into their own little waste basket.

296. Turn individual desks into dry erase boards with dry erase contact paper. Great for practice work so you don't waste paper.

297. Buy or make your own scratch-off tickets. Prizes could be bonus points, free time, excused tardy, etc.

298. If you see a store display you can use, ask the manager if they'll donate it to your classroom when they're done with it.

Chapter Fourteen

Recycling

Just Some Suggestions

299. Wash and rinse ketchup or jelly or shampoo bottles and fill with paint.

300. Save the coffee cups and fast food drinks that come with a domed lid. These are great no-spill containers for painting projects.

301. Decorate a Pringles canister then use it to store rulers or paint brushes.

302. Make a "Hydration Station" where kids can tuck their water bottles on the way in and pick them up on the way out by hanging a shoe caddy by the door.

Chapter Fifteen

Taxes

Records and Receipts

303. Save your receipts for all teaching supplies, resources or materials that were **not** paid for or reimbursed by your school.

304. Record teaching registration fees and related costs

305. If you're required to wear clothing with a school logo on it keep track of the costs as well as the cost of laundering it.

306. Add up all educational costs that relate to your current teaching position.

307. Some travel and meal expenses may be deductible if work related. Keep track.

308. Union and membership fees.

309. Work related books, magazines, journals, seminars, etc. Laws keep changing. Keep records.

310. The cost of your Internet and computer may be deductible if you work from home.

311. Keep all records and receipts separate for your tax agent.

Other Books

Our editor has written numerous other works. Please recommend Debra Chapoton to your students. She's written many young adult novels as well as books for kids 8 – 12. She has also published non-fiction products such as HOW TO HELP YOUR CHILD SUCCEED IN SCHOOL.

Fiction:

THE GIRL IN THE TIME MACHINE A desperate teen with a faulty time machine. What could go wrong? 17-year-old Laken is torn between revenge and righting a wrong. SciFi suspense.

THE TIME BENDER A stolen kiss could put the universe at risk. Selina doesn't think Marcum's spaceship is anything more than one heck of a science project ... until he takes her to the moon and back.

THE TIME PACER Alex discovered he was half-alien right after he learned how to manipulate time. Now he has to fight the star cannibals, fly a space ship, work on his relationship with Selina, and stay clear of Coreg, full-blooded alien rival and possible galactic traitor. Once they reach their ancestral planet all three are plunged into a society where schooling is more than indoctrination

THE TIME STOPPER Young recruit Marcum learns battle-craft, infiltration and multiple languages at the Interstellar Combat Academy. He and his arch rival Coreg jeopardize their futures by exceeding the space travel limits and flying to Earth in search of a time-bender. They find Selina whose ability to slow the passage of time will be invaluable in fighting other aliens. But Marcum loses his heart to her and when Coreg takes her twenty light years away he remains on Earth in order to develop a far greater talent than time-bending. Now he's ready to return home and get the girl.

THE TIME ENDER Selina Langston is confused about recurring feelings for the wrong guy/alien. She's pretty sure Alex is her soulmate and Coreg should not be trusted at all. But Marcum ... well, when he returns to Klaqin and rescues her she begins to see him in a different light.

EDGE OF ESCAPE Innocent adoration escalates to stalking and abduction in this psychological thriller. Also available in German, titled SOMMERFALLE.

THE GUARDIAN'S DIARY Jedidiah, a 17-year-old champion skateboarder with a defect he's been hiding all of his life, must risk exposure to rescue a girl that's gone missing.

SHELTERED Ben, a high school junior, has found a unique way to help homeless teens, but he must first bring the group together to fight against supernatural forces.

A SOUL'S KISS When a tragic accident leaves Jessica comatose, her spirit escapes her body. Navigating a supernatural realm is tough, but being half dead has its advantages. Like getting into people's thoughts. Like taking over someone's body. Like experiencing romance on a whole new plane - literally.

EXODIA By 2093 American life is a strange mix of failing technologies, psychic predictions, and radiation induced abilities. Tattoos are mandatory to differentiate two classes, privileged and slave. Dalton Battista fears that his fading tattoo is a deadly omen. He's either the heir of the brutal tyrant of the new capital city, Exodia, or he's its prophesied redeemer.

OUT OF EXODIA In this sequel to EXODIA, Dalton Battista takes on his prophesied identity as Bram O'Shea. When this psychic teen leads a city of 21st century American survivalists out from under an oppressive regime, he puts the escape plan at risk by trusting the mysterious god-like David Ronel.

Children's Books:

THE SECRET IN THE HIDDEN CAVE 12-year-old Missy Stark and her new friend Kevin Jackson discover dangerous secrets when they explore the old lodge, the woods, the cemetery, and the dark caves beneath the lake. They must solve the riddles and follow the clues to save the old lodge from destruction.

MYSTERY'S GRAVE After Missy and Kevin solved THE SECRET IN THE HIDDEN CAVE, they thought the rest of the summer at Big Pine Lodge would be normal. But there are plenty of surprises awaiting them in the woods, the caves, the stables, the attic and the cemetery. Two new families arrive and one family isn't human.

BULLIES AND BEARS In their latest adventure at Big Pine Lodge, Missy and Kevin discover more secrets in the caves, the attic, the cemetery and the settlers' ruins. They have to stay one step ahead of four teenage bullies, too, as well as three hungry bears. This summer's escapades become more and more challenging for these two twelve-year-olds. How will they make it through another week?

A TICK IN TIME 12-year-old Tommy MacArthur plunges into another dimension thanks to a magical grandfather clock. Now he must find his way through a strange land, avoid the danger lurking around every corner, and get back home. When he succeeds he dares his new friend Noelle to return with him, but who and what follows them back means more trouble and more adventure.

BIGFOOT DAY, NINJA NIGHT When 12-year-old Anna skips the school fair to explore the woods with Callie, Sydney, Austin, and Natalie, they find evidence of Bigfoot. No way! It looks like his tracks are following them. But that's not the worst part. And neither is stumbling upon Bigfoot's shelter. The worst part is they get separated and now they can't find Callie or the path that leads back to the school.

In the second story Luke and his brother, Nick, go on a boys only camping trip, but things get weird and scary very quickly. Is there a ninja in the woods with them? Mysterious things happen as day turns into night.

Non-fiction:

HOW TO BLEND FAMILIES A guide for stepparents

HOW TO HELP YOUR CHILD SUCCEED AT SCHOOL A guide for parents

BUILDING BIG PINE LODGE A journal of our experiences building a full log home

CROSSING THE SCRIPTURES A Bible Study supplement for studying each of the 66 books of the Old and New Testaments.

Author's website: bigpinelodgebooks.com